P7

SCIENCE WORKSHOP

WHEELS
PULLEYS & LEVERS

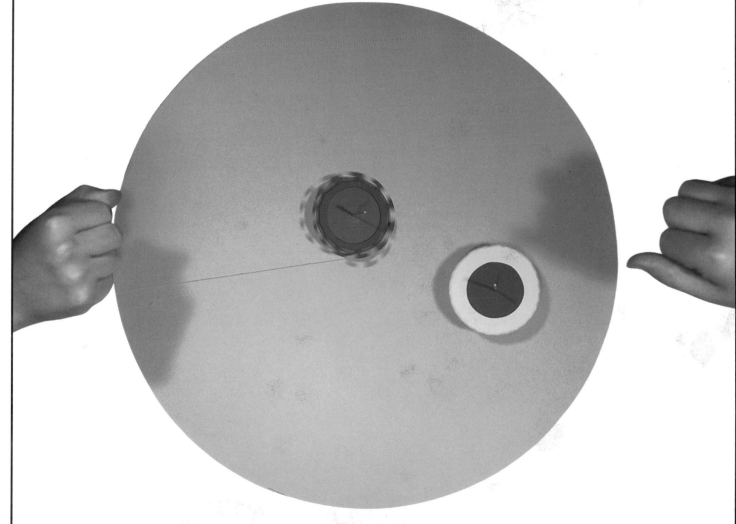

MICK SELLER

A WATTS BOOK

LONDON NEW YORK SYDNEY

Design   David West
                      Children's Book Design
Designer   Keith Newell
Editor   Suzanne Melia
Picture Researcher   Emma Krikler
Illustrators   Ian Thompson
Consultant   Bryson Gore

© Aladdin Books Ltd 1993
Created and designed by
N. W. Books
28 Percy Street
London W1P 9FF

First published in
Great Britain in 1993 by
Watts Books
96 Leonard Street
London EC2A 4RH

ISBN 0 7496 1175 8

A CIP catalogue record for this book
is available from the British Library

CONTENTS

PHOTOCREDITS

All the photographs in this book are by Roger
Vlitos apart from pages; 4 top, 10 top & 12
top: Spectrum Colour Library; 8 top: Dan
Brooks; 14 top: Eye Ubiquitous.

INTRODUCTION

Movement has always been an important part of human life. People need to move themselves around, and to move objects from one place to another. Throughout history, people searched for ways to make this movement faster and easier. In this search, simple machines were developed – not the complicated inventions that the word "machine" usually conjures up, but basic devices like wheels, levers , pulleys, screws and slopes. Not all of these could strictly be called inventions. Levers were present in the bodies of people and animals long before the concept of the lever was ever understood. Others, like the wheel, were invented over the course of thousands of years. All around us, in a walk to school or a trip around the local shopping centre, we see examples of these simple machines – all designed to make jobs easier for us. Much of the science of physics concerns the effort, or force, it takes to move an object, and investigates ways in which the same object can be moved with less effort. As you work your way through this book, you will learn about the inventions and discoveries which have made our modern, mechanical world the place it is today.

Why It Works explaining
science ideas

Introduction

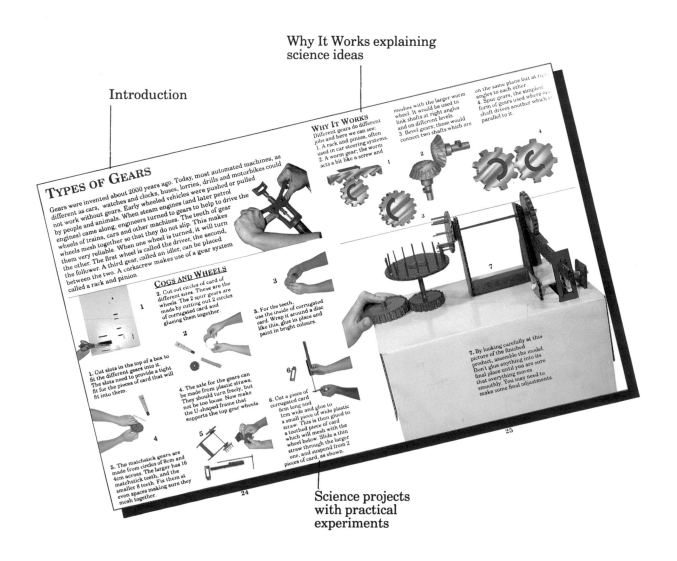

Science projects
with practical
experiments

THE WORKSHOP

A science workshop is a place to test ideas, perform experiments and make discoveries. To prove many scientific facts, you don't need a lot of fancy equipment. In fact, everything you need for a basic workshop can be found around your home or school. Read through these pages, and then use your imagination to add to your "home laboratory". As you work your way through this book, you should enjoy completing the projects and seeing your models work. Remember, though, that from a scientific point of view, these projects are just the starting point. For example, when you finish making the "shover" on pages 8/9, ask your own questions like "What would happen if I oiled the surface?", "Would a larger object move more slowly?", and so on. Also by sharing ideas, you will learn more. Experimenting with equipment, as well as with ideas, will give you the most accurate results. In this way, you will build up your workshop as you go along.

MAKING MODELS

Before you begin, read through all the steps. Then, make a list of the things you need and collect them together. Next, think about the project so that you have a clear idea of what you are about to do. Finally, take your time in putting the pieces together. You will find that your projects work best if you wait while glue or paint dries. If something goes wrong, retrace your steps. And, if you can't fix it, start over again. Every scientist makes mistakes, but the best ones know when to begin again!

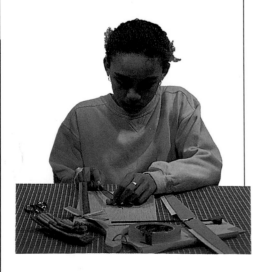

SAFETY WARNINGS

Make sure that an adult knows what you are doing at all times. Cutting the top off a plastic bottle can be difficult and dangerous if you use sharp scissors. Ask an adult to do this for you. Always be careful with balloons and plastic bags. Never cover your face with them. If you spill any water, wipe it up right away. Slippery surfaces are dangerous. Clean up after you have finished.

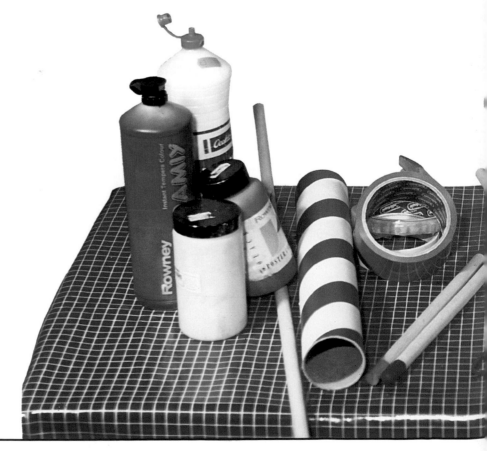

GENERAL TIPS

There are at least two parts to every experiment: experimenting with materials and testing a science "fact". If you don't have all the materials, experiment with others instead. For example, if you can't find any thick card, stick several layers together instead. Once you've finished experimenting, read your notes thoroughly and think about what happened, evaluating your measurements and observations. What conclusions can you draw from your results?

EXPERIMENTING

Always conduct a "fair test". This means changing one thing at a time for each stage of an experiment. In this way, you can always tell which change caused a different result. As you go along, record what you see. Ask questions such as "why?", "how?" and "what if?". Then test your model and write down the answers you arrive at.

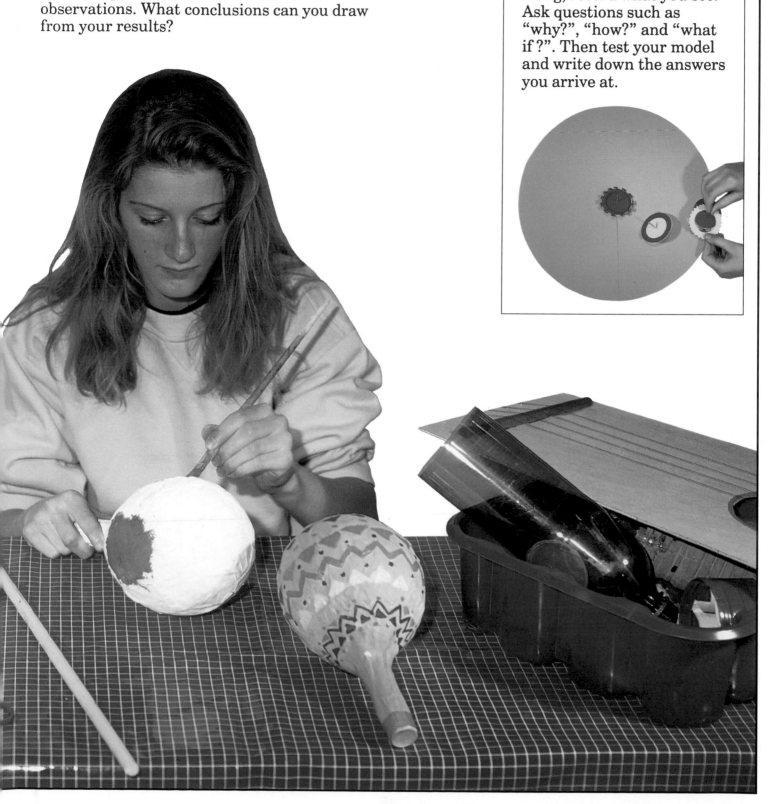

LOAD AND EFFORT

Imagine climbing to the top of a steep hill on a hot day. Think about what hard work it would be. Next, try to picture yourself climbing to the same height on a more gentle slope. It would take longer, but you would not find it such hard work. The gentler slope, or gradient, allows you to climb to the same height by using less effort. The slope is, in fact, acting as a simple and basic machine which makes work easier. You may think of a machine as a complicated device in a factory, but actually a slope, or inclined plane, to give it its proper name, is one of the oldest machines known to man. Stairs are a series of slopes which allow us to climb with relatively little effort.

BRIGHT IDEAS

Cut out a paper triangle and starting with the thin end of the wedge wrap it around a pencil. Does the shape remind you of a screw? A screw is a bit like a slope which is going round and round in a spiral.

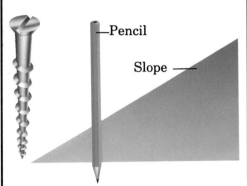

—Pencil

Slope —

PULLING POWER

1

2. Build a solid frame from straws, and reinforce it with card. Stick them together with tape and then join the frame to the ramp.

2

1. Make a slope from stiff card. Cut out and score along the edges, as shown. Fold, and stick with glue. Keep this slope safely, you will need to use it in later projects.

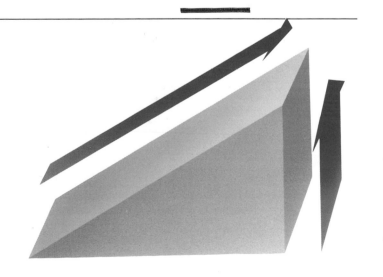

WHY IT WORKS

When the load (as the car being lifted would be called by scientists) is pulled up the ramp, it travels a longer distance than when it is brought up in the lift. If the weight of the car was 500 grammes, then an effort of 500g would be needed to pull it straight up in the lift. If an effort of 100g was needed to pull it up the slope, then we say that the ramp has a mechanical advantage of 500g divided by 100g which equals 5. In other words, without the slope you would need 5 times as much effort.

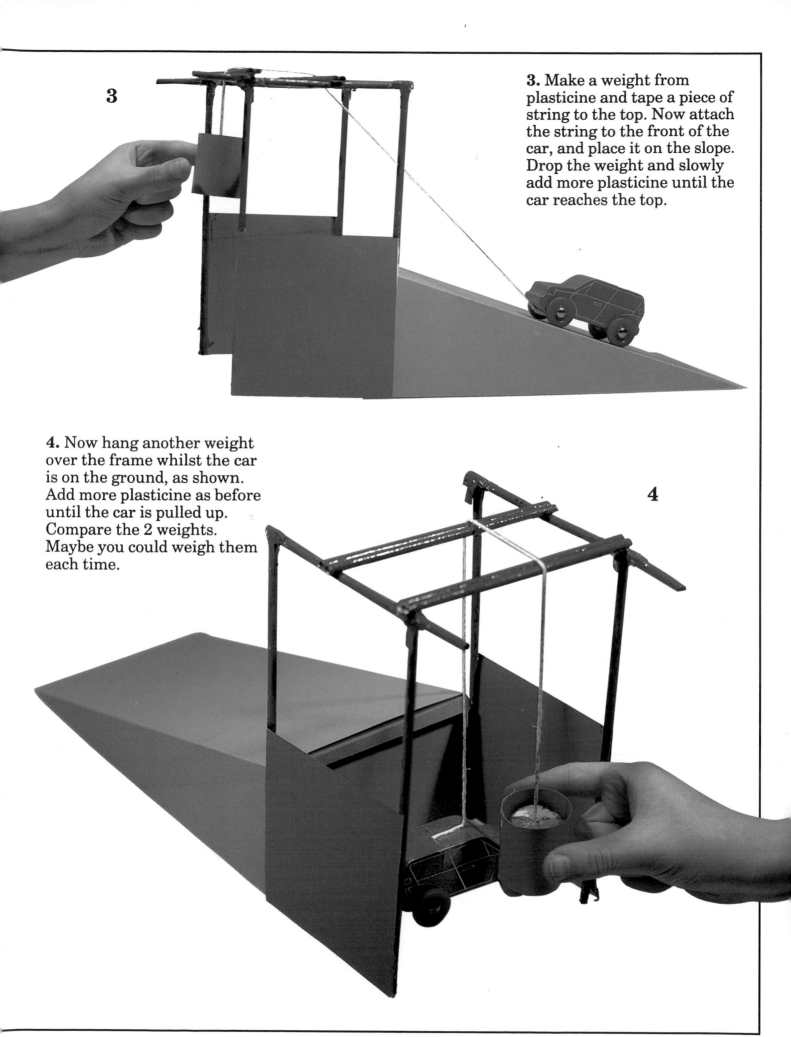

3. Make a weight from plasticine and tape a piece of string to the top. Now attach the string to the front of the car, and place it on the slope. Drop the weight and slowly add more plasticine until the car reaches the top.

4. Now hang another weight over the frame whilst the car is on the ground, as shown. Add more plasticine as before until the car is pulled up. Compare the 2 weights. Maybe you could weigh them each time.

MOVING THINGS

Have you ever tried to push a heavy box across the floor? If you have, you would have noticed that this can feel like hard work – especially if the box is heavy and the floor is rough. To a scientist, there are two reasons for this: the first is gravity – the force which pulls all things down to Earth and makes them feel heavy. The second reason is friction – the forces which are produced when the box begins to move and its surface rubs against the ground. Gravity and friction are the most common forces which stop things from moving. They oppose movement. If these forces were not acting on the box, it would carry on moving for ever when you gave it a push!

WHY IT WORKS

To make something move, we first have to apply a force – this means we have to push it, pull it, twist it, blow it and so on. When we pushed shapes with our "controlled shover", they moved a little way until the opposing forces of gravity and friction stopped them. In the diagram, you can see these forces acting against your push, or initial force.

5. Try shoving objects of different sizes and different materials. Some objects, like a marble, move further because their shape allows them to overcome the force

5

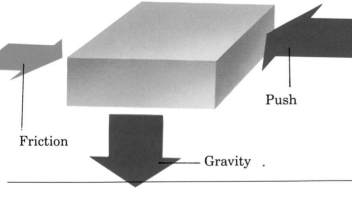

Friction

Push

Gravity .

BRIGHT IDEAS

Put your shover into a vertical position and try pushing the shapes again. The shapes do not have the same amount of friction working against them now. If you shoot each shape up with an equal shove, you will see there is much less difference in how far the shapes go.

Tie a brick up with string. Now pull it steadily along the floor using a spring balance. Try pulling other objects, and compare your readings.

SHOVE IT!

1. Cut out a long piece of card and paint it with equally spaced stripes. Stick a piece of straw to one end, as shown.

2. Join 2 thinner pieces of straw to make your shover. Place it inside the wide straw, lining it up with the first stripe. Push a small piece of stick through the straw to stop it moving forwards.

3. Now stretch a piece of elastic around the stick, and pin it to the board, as shown. You stretch this back when you prepare to fire.

4. Use the stick as a handle to pull your shover back. Pull it as far as it will go. Place an object in front and let go.

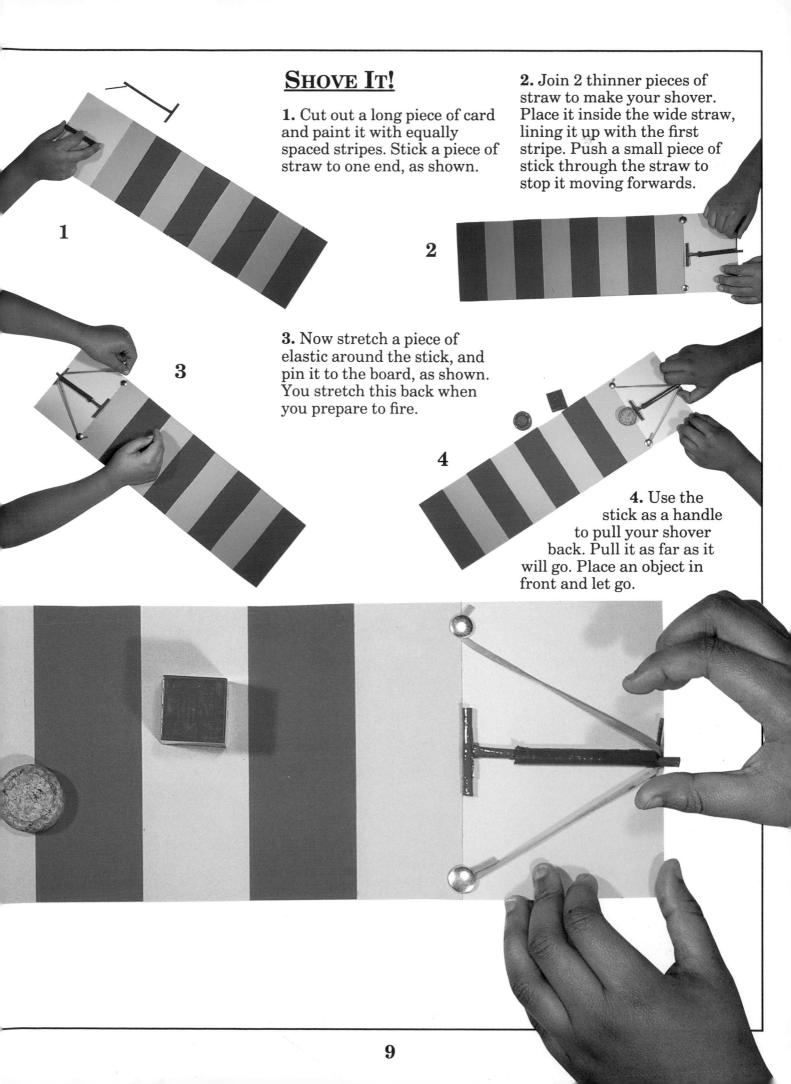

OVERCOMING FRICTION

Throughout history people have searched for easier ways to move things around. The builders of the Egyptian pyramids would have had to drag huge lumps of building stone for long distances. The forces of friction and gravity made this very hard work. They found, however, that by placing rollers under the stone blocks, they could drag the same block more efficiently. The rollers themselves would have simply been the trunks of trees. Round objects, like the ball-bearings pictured here, overcome the forces of friction and move easily.

SLIP SLIDING

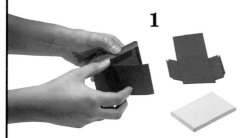

1

1. Make a car from card, as shown. Draw windows on the sides. Make a flat container from yellow card. It should be the same width as the car and about 3mm deep.

2. Fill the container with pieces of straw. These will behave like rollers. They should fit snuggly without being glued.

2

3

3. Use the slope you built on pages 6/7. The car, without rollers, marbles or wheels, will not move. Tip the ramp until the car slides down. It will have to go quite high.

4. Holding the straws in their box, turn it upside down and place at the top of the slope. Fit the car on top and let it go. Does the car move more easily with rollers?

4

5. Build 2 containers, wide enough for a row of marbles. Put the marbles in the containers. These will act as ball-bearings.

5

WHY IT WORKS

The car will not slide smoothly down the ramp without the rollers or marbles because friction stops it. The amount of friction (shown in red) depends on two things : the weight of the object which we want to move, and the kind of surfaces which the object and the floor have. The greater the weight, the harder the two surfaces are squeezed together, and the rougher the surface the more friction is created. Friction can be reduced by rolling an object rather than pushing or dragging it. The rollers and marbles roll underneath your car. There will be some friction, but a lot less than when the whole of the car itself was in contact with the ramp.

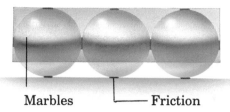

Flat surface — Friction

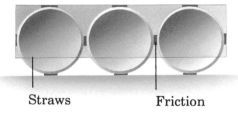

Marbles — Friction

Straws — Friction

BRIGHT IDEAS

☀ Try letting your car go down the ramp sideways. Does it move more easily with the straw rollers or the marbles?

☀ Change the surface of your ramp. Try sandpaper or a piece of carpet. What difference does this make to how well your car rolls?

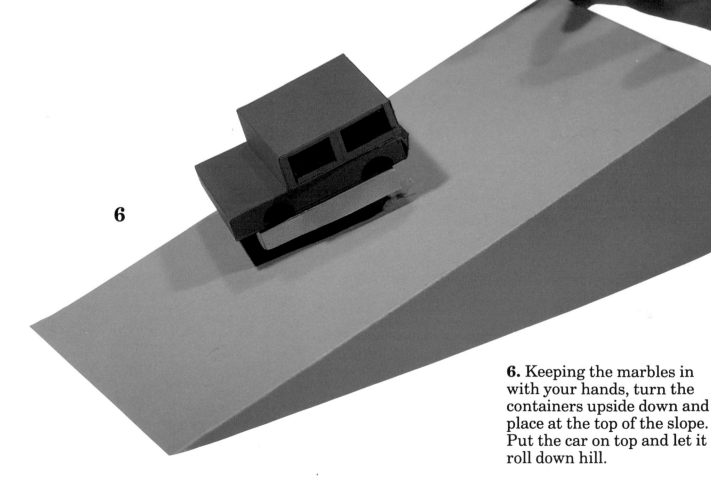

6

6. Keeping the marbles in with your hands, turn the containers upside down and place at the top of the slope. Put the car on top and let it roll down hill.

WHEEL AND AXLE

The earliest known wheels were made in ancient Mesopotamia around 3000 B.C. Early four-wheeled carts were not very practical though. Their wheels were fixed rigidly to the axles of the cart which made it very difficult for them to turn corners. About 2000 years ago, a front axle which could pivot was invented. In the Middle Ages, smaller front wheels combined with cutting away a small section of the body made steerable vehicles much better. Today, we have pressed steel and alloy wheels, pneumatic (air filled) tyres, spoked wheels and many others.

STEER CLEAR

2. Make the body of your car from card. Cut out a shape like this one, and stick the edges together. Leave a flap to cross underneath the car. This will hold the axle. Decorate with your own strip.

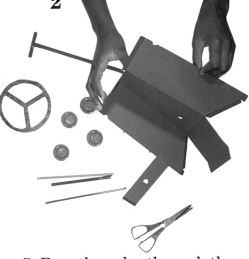

1. Build the main steering column for your car from a large straw. Fix a smaller piece of straw across one end to form the front axle holder.

4. Turn the car upside down and make a hole for the steering column to pass through. This can be reinforced with thick card.

5. Pass the axles through the thick straws and attach the other wheels. You can split the ends of the straws and glue them in place. Tape the other axle in position.

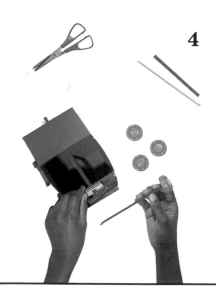

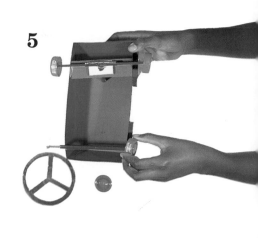

3. Make the axles from thin straws. These can be pushed through thicker straws and attached to the plastic bottle tops that are the car's wheels.

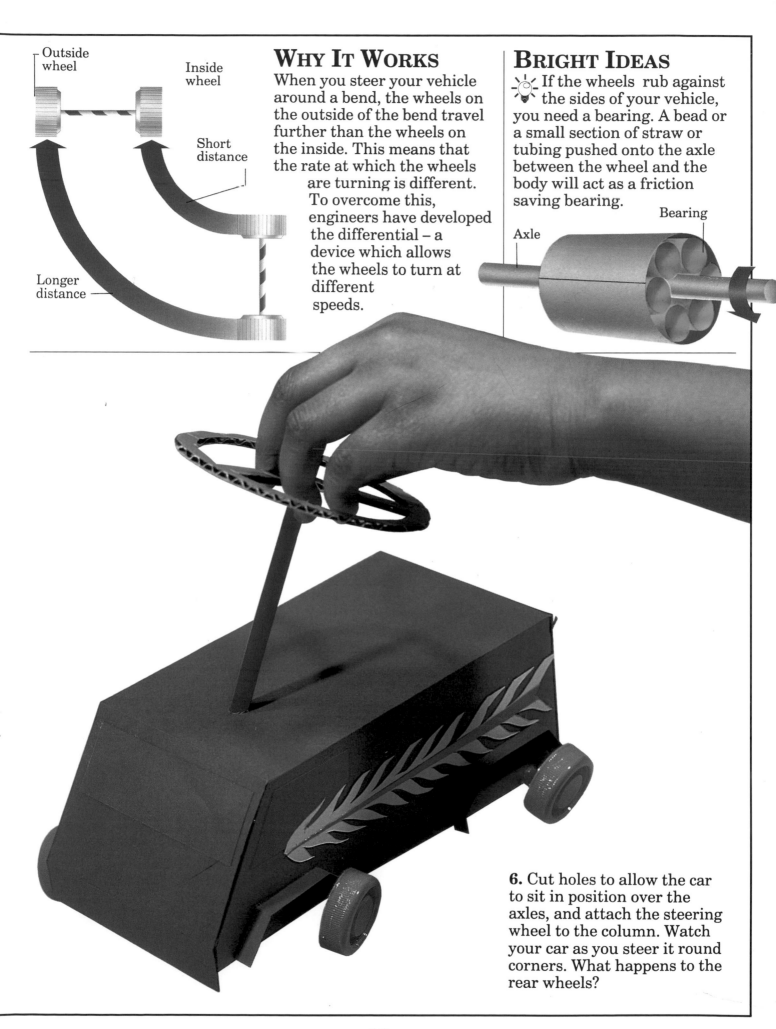

Outside wheel

Inside wheel

Short distance

Longer distance

WHY IT WORKS

When you steer your vehicle around a bend, the wheels on the outside of the bend travel further than the wheels on the inside. This means that the rate at which the wheels are turning is different. To overcome this, engineers have developed the differential – a device which allows the wheels to turn at different speeds.

BRIGHT IDEAS

If the wheels rub against the sides of your vehicle, you need a bearing. A bead or a small section of straw or tubing pushed onto the axle between the wheel and the body will act as a friction saving bearing.

Axle

Bearing

6. Cut holes to allow the car to sit in position over the axles, and attach the steering wheel to the column. Watch your car as you steer it round corners. What happens to the rear wheels?

13

USING FRICTION

Wheels, bearings and lubricants, like oil, have all been developed to reduce friction between moving parts. At other times, though, friction is very useful to us. For example, think of how difficult it is to walk on a slippery surface like ice or of how cars can crash when they lose their grip on wet or oily roads. In cases like this, special shoes or car tyres are designed to cause friction and so give grip. Many tyres have been developed to give grip. Huge knobbly tyres help tractors and earth-movers to drive on rough and slippery ground.

NO OBSTACLE!

1. Your tank will be powered by a cotton-reel and elastic band which can be wound up. Energy is stored in the twisted elastic band and released slowly as the tank crawls along.

1

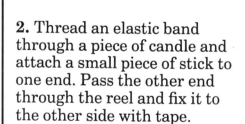

2. Thread an elastic band through a piece of candle and attach a small piece of stick to one end. Pass the other end through the reel and fix it to the other side with tape.

2

3

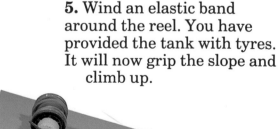

3. Cut a piece of card to this shape, making sure the semi-circles are big enough to fit over a cotton-reel. The body of the tank shouldn't touch the surface.

5. Wind an elastic band around the reel. You have provided the tank with tyres. It will now grip the slope and climb up.

4

4. Wind the stick as tight as it will go, and place the reel at the bottom of the slope. Will it travel up quite easily?

5

WHY IT WORKS

For your cotton reel tank, friction is both a good and a bad thing. The material which you wrap around the reel, for example elastic bands or sandpaper, creates a large amount of friction as the tank moves up the slope, and this gives grip. Without this grip, the tank would probably slip and fail to climb the slope. When the stick rubs against the reel, however, the friction caused here makes the tank less efficient, and slows it down. The disc of candle wax comes between the rough surfaces and acts as both a bearing and a lubricant, and allows the stick to turn more easily against the reel. Surfaces with an uneven texture (1) cause friction when objects move over them. If lubricants, like oil, are applied to the surface, the valleys and holes are filled in (2). The surface becomes smooth, and friction is greatly reduced. The surface may be slippery.

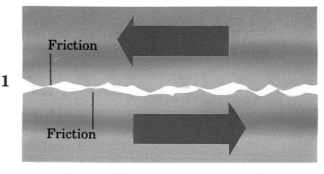

1

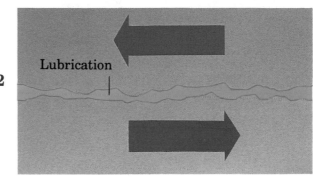

2

---

6. Stick the tank shape together, and carefully place over the reel. It doesn't need to be fixed. A straw or pencil can be the tank's gun.

BRIGHT IDEAS

☀ Make your slope steeper. What is the steepest slope the cotton reel tank will climb?
☀ Experiment with different elastic bands. Which bands are better for hill climbing – thick or thin?
☀ Try your tank on different surfaces. Can you see how rough surfaces create more friction and help your tank to climb? Lubricate the surface with wax or oil. Does it slow the tank down?

6

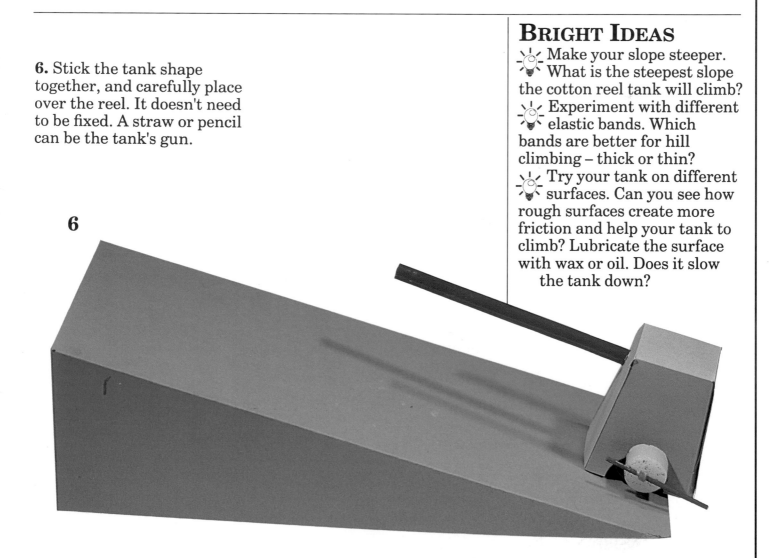

SPINNING WHEELS

So many things rely on wheels apart from cars and other vehicles. A fairground would not be much fun without wheels. A roundabout in a playground is a large spinning wheel. When a wheel is made to spin, as long as there is nothing rubbing against it, it will continue to spin for a long time. Scientists, engineers and even toy-makers have made use of this fact in many situations. Inside a car engine, there is a heavy wheel which spins when the engine is running and even after it's turned off. This wheel is the flywheel, and it helps the car to run smoothly.

BATTLING TOPS

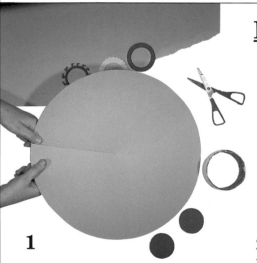

1. Cut out a large circle of card about 40 cm across. This is the "arena" for the battle. Also cut out three small circles of 4 cm across.

2. Cut a slit from the edge of the large circle to the middle. Cross the edges to make a cone shape and fix underneath with tape.

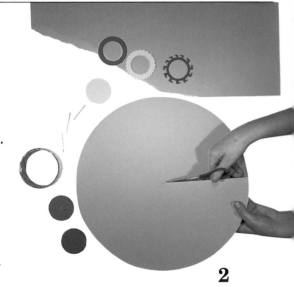

3. Turn the cone upside down, and stand the point in a circle of strong card. The inside of a thick roll of sticky-tape will do.

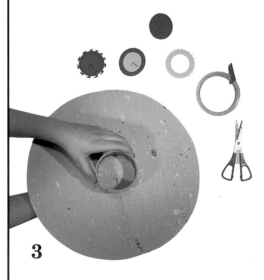

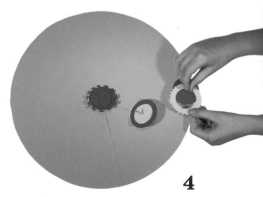

4. Decorate your tops with rings of coloured card, and push sharpened matchsticks through the centre of each.

WHY IT WORKS

When we set the battling tops spinning, we have to give them a sharp twist. The greater the twist, the longer the top will spin. The energy of the initial twist is not all used up straight away, some of it is stored within the top. The gradual release of this energy is what keeps the top going. The top acts as a kind of flywheel. You can find examples of flywheels in toys which have "friction motors." By winding the back wheels of the car on the ground, energy is stored in the flywheel.

Flywheel

Movement of car

BRIGHT IDEAS

Hold the wheel of a bicycle so it can turn freely and set it spinning. The wheel will carry on spinning, using up the stored energy. Be careful not to put your fingers near the spokes of the wheel!

5. Spin the tops, dropping them onto your cone. Make sure the sticks are exactly through the centre or they won't spin properly. Watch them battle in the arena.

5

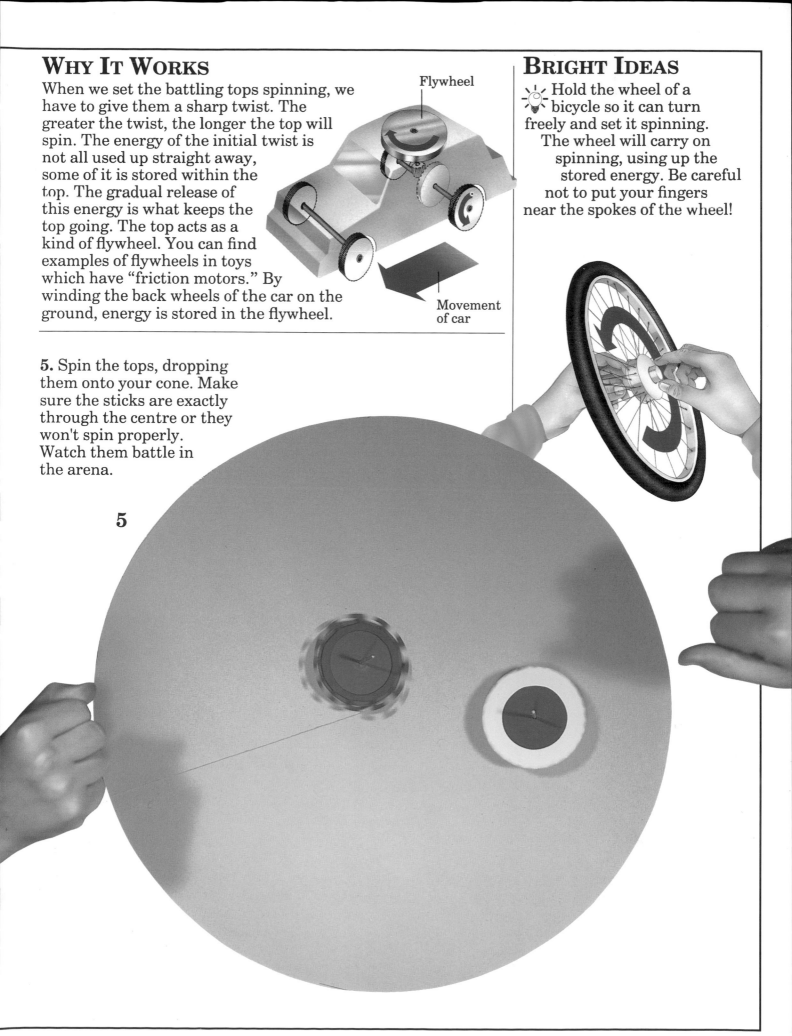

WINCHES AND WHEELS

One important use of wheels is in harnessing the power of wind and water, and using the energy to perform useful jobs. Water wheels, like this one, were designed to capture the energy of running water, and transfer it into energy to power machinery. Turbines are modern water wheels which turn in streams of water released from behind dams, and generate electricity. Old fashioned windmills used the energy of the wind for grinding corn, while modern windmills are commonly used for pumping water. Another important wheel is a winch. This is a special roller which is used to make the lifting of heavy loads an easier task.

BRIGHT IDEAS

- ☀ Try using your cotton reel tank to lift up weights (below). You would have to work out the best way to fix it to a table top first.
- ☀ Using a cork and four pieces of thin plastic you could make your own water wheel. Make 4 notches in the cork and insert the pieces of plastic. If you attach it to a piece of wood so it turns, you could make a paddle boat.
- ☀ Have you got a toy seaside windmill? If you have you could modify it to make it lift a small weight when the wind blows on it.

7. Wind your thread and bucket around the reel. Now all you need is the wind to raise and lower it. Produce this by blowing through a straw.

7

WHY IT WORKS

The energy which you use to blow the sails around, provides the force to turn your wind-powered winch. If you tried to move the weight by blowing underneath it, you would have little chance of succeeding. The winch, however, makes it possible to lift the weight by blowing in the following way. Pulling a weight up a steep slope will take more effort than pulling it up a gentle one (remember chapter 1?) Although the force, or effort, is less, it is applied for a greater distance. In effect, by blowing onto the tips of the sails you apply the force for a great distance in order to lift the weight over a very short one. The tip of the sail will probably travel 10m to lift the weight 10cm. The work of lifting the weight is therefore made much easier.

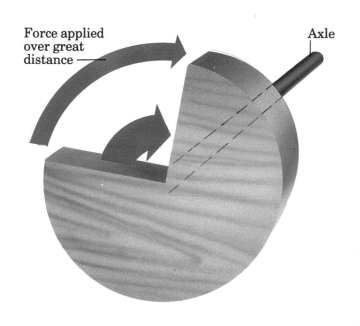

Force applied over great distance

Axle

WIND POWER

1

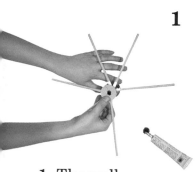

1. The well makes it possible to raise a bucket using "wind power". Stick 6 straws to the end of a cotton reel leaving the centre clear. Secure with a piece of card.

4

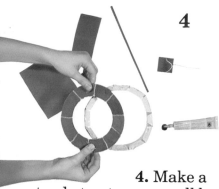

4. Make a sturdy top to your wall by painting a ring of card. Make 2 holes for the upright supports.

2. Make a little bucket from card, and attach to a long piece of string. The string passes through 2 holes in the top of the bucket, so it hangs level.

2

5. To suspend your wheel between 2 posts, thread a straw through the centre of the reel for your axle and fix the 2 ends through 2 large straws. Fit into the top of the wall.

5

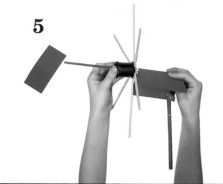

3

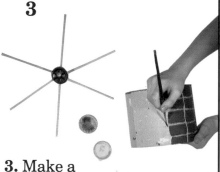

3. Make a base for your well from card and decorate it to give a brick effect. The top of the wall can be made by cutting slits and folding the card over.

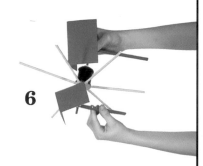

6

6. The posts should be long enough to stand in the wall, giving the wheel room to turn. Add 2 little roofs made from V-shaped pieces of card.

PULLEY SYSTEMS

If you have ever had a chance to watch a crane at work, you were probably amazed by the enormous weights which it could lift. Cranes can be seen on building sites, on ships and docksides, in railway yards, on the backs of lorries – the list could go on. Cranes make lifting easier by using powerful winding engines and pulleys (special wheels shaped so that ropes and wires are kept in place as they move). Pulley systems can be very simple, like the block and tackle pictured here. A builder standing on the ground might use a rope and a single pulley fixed to the top of a building to lift a bucket of cement to a friend working above. This would be a lot less effort than climbing a ladder with the bucket.

BRIGHT IDEAS

💡 Make a simple "fixed pulley" system of your own using cotton reels, wire loops and string.

💡 A special pulley, called a block and tackle, is used for lifting heavy loads, for example on building sites. This device has a set of pulley wheels which means the lifting force has to be applied for a tremendous distance in order to lift a load just a little way. Look at the sketch, and by using coat hangers and cotton reels have a go at making your own block and tackle.

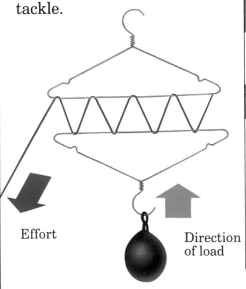

Effort

Direction of load

PULL TOGETHER

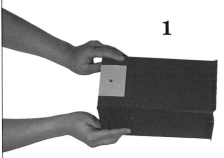

1

2. Push a thin straw through the box. At the centre, suspend a cotton reel with two pieces of straw either side to keep it central.

3

4. Bend some coat-hanger wire, and attach it to the cotton reels as the picture of the crane on the opposite page shows. Suspend from a hook at the end of the arm.

1. Make a tall tower from card, as shown, leaving it open at the top and bottom. Reinforce one side and make a hole for the winch to pass through.

2

3. Make an arm for the crane from card, and fix to the main part with glue. Stick a small piece of straw underneath the arm at the end to guide the string over the cotton reels.

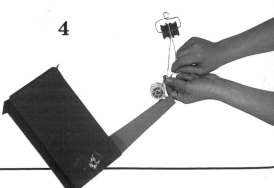

4

WHY IT WORKS

A pulley system allows a small force to be applied over a long distance. When a force moves an object, scientists say that work is being done. Work is measured in units called joules, and is equal to the force which you apply, multiplied by the distance the load is lifted. With a single pulley system (right), the load moves the same distance as the rope pulled in. It doesn't amplify (or help increase) the effort. In a double pulley system (far right), the load moves only half the distance of the rope pulled in. Distance is halved and the force raising the load is double the effort pulling the rope.

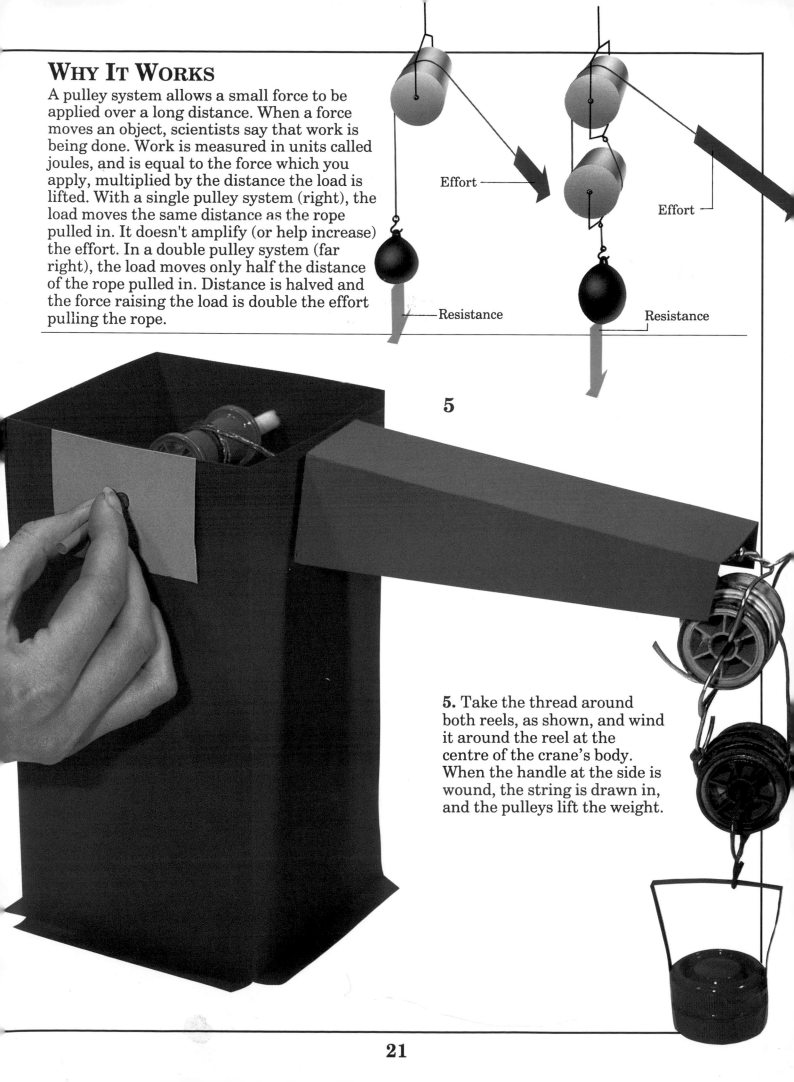

Effort

Effort

Resistance

Resistance

5

5. Take the thread around both reels, as shown, and wind it around the reel at the centre of the crane's body. When the handle at the side is wound, the string is drawn in, and the pulleys lift the weight.

GEARS

Today's cyclists have a much easier time than the men and women who rode the very first bicycles over 100 years ago. The draisienne was a popular cycle in 1820 – but it was a heavy thing without pedals; you had to free wheel along, like you would on a scooter! About 1885, J.K. Starley produced the first commercially successful safety bicycle with pedals which used a chain to drive the rear wheel, leaving the front wheel free for steering. The bicycle continued to improve, and today modern machines make climbing steep hills and travelling at high speeds possible by the clever use of special, toothed wheels, called gears.

BRIGHT IDEAS

Turn your bicycle upside-down and turn the pedals slowly to make the wheels turn. Be careful not to trap your fingers. By pushing a piece of paper into the spokes when the wheel is still, you will be able to count how many times the wheel turns for each full turn of the pedals. Change gear and count again.

6. When both feet are attached to the bike, one leg should be up when the other is down. The left foot should be fixed to the keyhole shaped cam, not directly to the pedal wheel. The front wheel can also be fixed with a fastener.

6

22

PEDAL POWER

1. Draw a template of your cyclist. The body of the cyclist and the frame are one piece. The wheels and the cyclist's legs are separate.

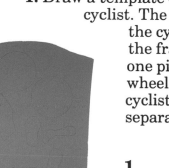

1

WHY IT WORKS

As we turn the pedals on a bike, the large pedal gear turns the smaller gear wheel on the back wheel by means of the chain. In the bottom picture, if the pedal gear has 50 teeth and the rear gear has 10 teeth then the wheel will turn five times for every turn of the pedals. This is called a high gear and would be best for going fast on flat ground. In the top picture, if the rear gear also has 50 teeth, it will only turn once for every turn of the pedals. This is a low gear and would be good for climbing hills.

2. Paint your pieces realistically. The back wheel is made up of 3 separate discs of thick card, held with a paper fastener. The smallest 2 are your gear wheels.

2

Pedal wheel

Low gear

High gear

Pedal wheel

3

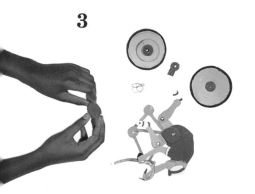

3. Join the legs of the cyclist at the knee and the hip. Cut out a thick piece of card, 3 cm across. It should be thick enough to support an elastic band. The cyclist's foot will pedal this around.

5

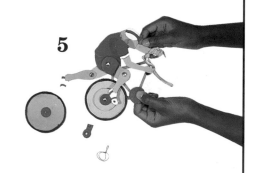

4

4. Attach the disc to the bike with a piece of stick, so it turns. A small cam (the blue keyhole shape) is attached to the straw on the other side, and then to the other foot with a fastener.

5. Attach an elastic band from the back wheel to the pedal wheel. As the back wheel turns, the cyclist's legs will begin to pedal. If the elastic is moved to the smaller gear, the cyclist will pedal even faster.

TYPES OF GEARS

Gears were invented about 2000 years ago. Today, most automated machines, as different as cars, watches and clocks, buses, lorries, drills and motorbikes could not work without gears. Early wheeled vehicles were pushed or pulled by people and animals. When steam engines (and later petrol engines) came along, engineers turned to gears to help to drive the wheels of trains, cars and other machines. The teeth of gear wheels mesh together so that they do not slip. This makes them very reliable. When one wheel is turned, it will turn the other. The first wheel is called the driver, the second, the follower. A third gear, called an idler, can be placed between the two. A corkscrew makes use of a gear system called a rack and pinion.

COGS AND WHEELS

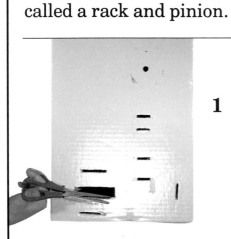

1

2. Cut out circles of card of different sizes. These are the wheels. The 2 spur gears are made by cutting out 2 circles of corrugated card and glueing them together.

2

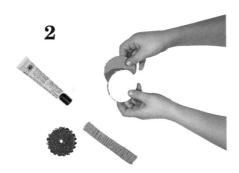

3

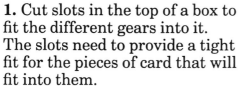

3. For the teeth, use the inside of corrugated card. Wrap it around a disc like this, glue in place and paint in bright colours.

1. Cut slots in the top of a box to fit the different gears into it. The slots need to provide a tight fit for the pieces of card that will fit into them.

4

5. The matchstick gears are made from circles of 8cm and 4cm across. The larger has 16 matchstick teeth, and the smaller 8 teeth. Fix them at even spaces making sure they mesh together.

4. The axle for the gears can be made from plastic straws. They should turn freely, but not be too loose. Now make the U-shaped frame that supports the top gear wheels.

5

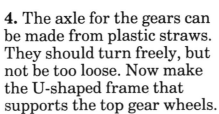

6

6. Cut a piece of corrugated card 6cm long and 1cm wide and glue to a small piece of wide plastic straw. This is then glued to a toothed piece of card which will mesh with the wheel below. Slide a thin straw through the larger one, and suspend from 2 pieces of card, as shown.

WHY IT WORKS

Different gears do different jobs and here we can see:
1. A rack and pinion, often used in car steering systems.
2. A worm gear; the worm acts a bit like a screw and meshes with the larger worm wheel. It would be used to link shafts at right angles and on different levels.
3. Bevel gears; these would connect two shafts which are on the same plane but at right angles to each other.
4. Spur gears, the simplest form of gears used where one shaft drives another which is parallel to it.

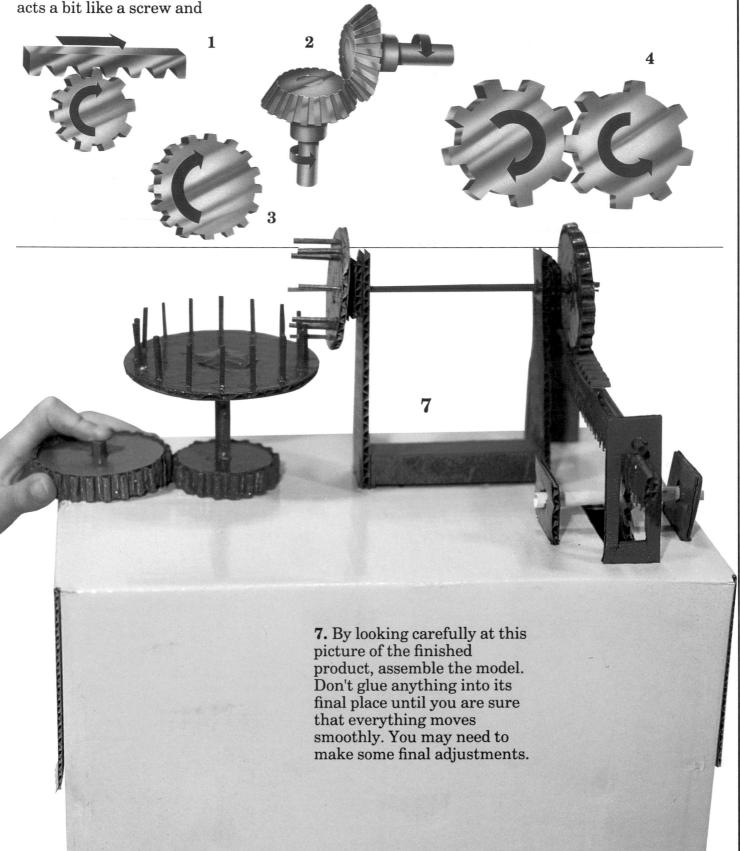

7. By looking carefully at this picture of the finished product, assemble the model. Don't glue anything into its final place until you are sure that everything moves smoothly. You may need to make some final adjustments.

LEVERS

As we have seen before, machines are devices which make work easier. There are five basic machines: the wheel and axle, the inclined plane or wedge, the pulley, the screw and the lever. If you think about someone moving a heavy rock with the help of a crowbar, you can picture a lever making a difficult job easier. We use levers in countless ways; brake levers on cycles, scissors, nutcrackers, a spanner, and a pair of pliers are examples of levers. In each case levers make work easier. In our bodies too, levers are at work making everyday movements like biting, running, throwing and kicking more effective.

FULL FORCE

5. Attach the hand and hammer to a piece of thick card as shown, and make a pivot from 3 pieces of straw. Balance it as shown here. Now, set up all the pieces like this, making sure that when the see-saw is activated, the hand pushes the shoot up, the marble rolls down the channel and falls onto the lever. You may need to try it a few times to position all the pieces correctly. When everything is in the right place, glue the parts down and insert the paper-fastener ready for hammering home.

5

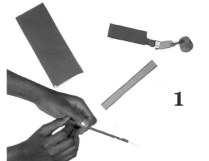

1. Make the see-saw from card. A piece of straw can act as a pivot. Attach a long straw to one end.

2. Make a tall box from card, and bend another piece into a shoot for the marble.

3. Glue the shoot to the top of the box, as shown, and attach a small hand to the end of the straw.

4. Make a small hammer from a straw and a piece of cork. It will fit into another card hand-shape.

WHY IT WORKS

First class levers (1) pivot on a fulcrum (red) between the effort (blue) and the load (yellow) (like a crowbar or a pair of scissors). Second class levers (2) place the load between the fulcrum and the effort (like a pair of nut-crackers). Third class levers (3) are ones where the effort is applied between the fulcrum and the load (As in some sugar tongs or in lifting a fish out of the water with a fishing rod). The purple arrow is resistance.

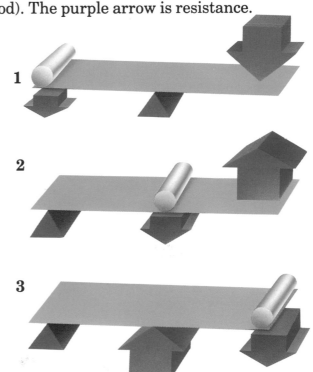

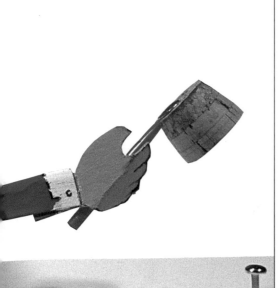

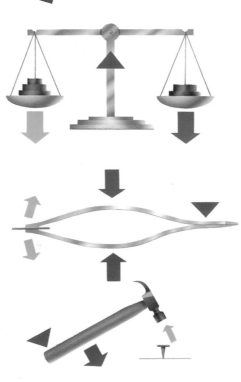

BRIGHT IDEAS

Can you tell which class each lever in the pictures fits into? The green arrows indicate resistance, the blue arrows are the effort, the red triangles are the fulcrum.

Use a lever to lift a weight. Put a small building brick under a ruler for a fulcrum, and place a weight on one end of it. Push down on the other end of the ruler. Now move the brick closer to the weight and push again. You will have to push for longer, and the weight will not move as far, but do you notice how it takes less effort to move the weight?

LEVERS IN PAIRS

In many tools and machines, levers work together in pairs, and the fulcrum (the place where the levers pivot) is often at the point where the levers are fixed together. Pliers, nutcrackers, scissors and tweezers are all examples of levers working in pairs. In the human body, there are many instances of levers working in pairs. Think about the strength of a bite which is produced by your jaw muscles pulling your jaws together. Your jaws are actually working as levers. Also when you grip something between your thumb and forefinger, look at the way they close together – your bones are levers.

GRAB THAT!

1. Cut out the card shapes shown here to make your mechanical grabber. The body of the crane is made from 2 cardboard boxes. Paint it lots of bright colours.

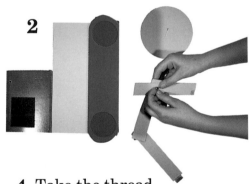

3. The teeth of the grabber are made from 2 pieces of card. The top one is stuck to the arm and the bottom one is fixed to the top half with a fastener. Only the bottom of the "jaw" moves. Attach a match stick to the top set of teeth, and tie a long piece of thread to it.

2. Make the moving arm from 3 pieces of card. The top 2 pieces should be fixed together with a fastener so it pivots. Cut a circle of card about 10cm across for your turntable. It is fixed to the crane with a pin so it moves.

4. Take the thread down the arm, through 2 bits of straw which are guides. The end of the thread is tied to a straw which can be wound around like a handle. Staple an elastic band between the bottom set of teeth and the arm.

5. The elastic should keep the jaws of the grabber open. When the handle is wound, the thread tightens, pulling the bottom "jaw" towards the top, closing them.

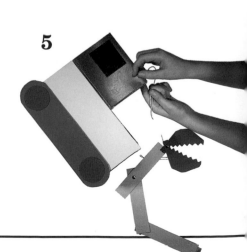

WHY IT WORKS

Effort

Resistance

Fulcrum

Levers working in a pair are most useful for gripping, cutting and squeezing jobs. The jaws of the grabber close together like those of a pair of pliers or like those of a dog. The force applied to each lever is increased by the effect of the lever at the point where the jaws meet, and because two sets of forces are being applied at this point the force of the grip is very strong. A pair of scissors is a compound first-class lever. It produces a strong cutting action very near the fulcrum (red). The load is the resistance of the fabric to the cutting blades. The green arrows indicate resistance. In the bottle-opener, pushing the handle up overcomes the strong resistance of a bottle cap. The effort is shown with blue arrows.

Fulcrum

Effort

Resistance

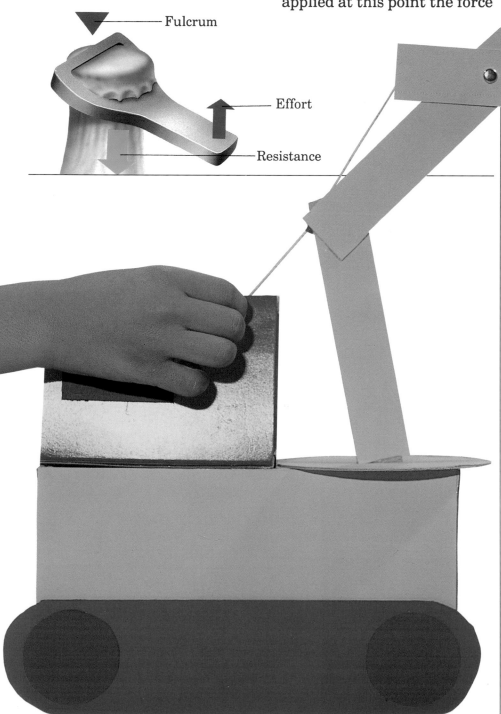

BRIGHT IDEAS

💡 Can you make your own model grabbing hand? You could make something like the grabber, but with fingers.

💡 Hold the muscles of your right fore-arm and clench your right fist. Can you feel them contracting and working the levers of your hand?

💡 Bend a nail with your own hands! You'll need two pieces of pipe, each one about 20cm long. Put a long nail into one piece of pipe so that half of its length sticks out. Place the other piece of pipe over this half of the nail. By applying a downward force to the ends of the piece of pipe you should be able to bend the nail quite easily.

COMPLEX MACHINES

Wheels, gears, pulleys and levers have developed over the course of thousands of years. Today, the science of engineering uses these simple machines in incredibly complex and precise ways. Many modern pieces of design, use a combination of simple machines, for example a bicycle. Spoked wheels with pneumatic tyres combine with gears and chain wheels to drive the cycle along. The pedals of a bicycle, gear change levers and the brakes, all use the principle of levers to make work easier, and the gear change cables are often guided by pulleys. Everyday objects, like clocks and watches, contain a complex series of wheels and levers.

WHY IT WORKS

At its most simple... the finger pushes the see-saw... the hand on the see-saw pushes the shoot... the marble rolls off the shoot and hits the second see-saw... this raises the box which holds the bobbin... the box tips as its front hits the second shoot... the bobbin rolls down the shoot and strikes the hammer... and the hammer hits the mouse! (Apologies to animal lovers everywhere).

6. The bullet shape is a plasticine counter weight wrapped in card - this should balance with the bobbin and box EXACTLY. Set up your mouse-trap by placing the box on the end of the small see-saw and the marble on the middle of the top shoot... Now just wait for a mouse.

6

BRIGHT IDEAS

💡 Can you modify your mouse-trap so that the mouse landing on the cheese activates the mouse trap?

💡 If you have a construction set which has sets of gears, experiment and try to make a conveyor belt which will take a parcel around a corner.

💡 Convert your mouse-trap design to a burglar alarm which rings a warning (when the hammer hits a small bell) when someone enters your bedroom.

💡 Take the back off a watch or clock and have a close look at the mechanism. How many different wheels and levers can you see?

TRAPPED!

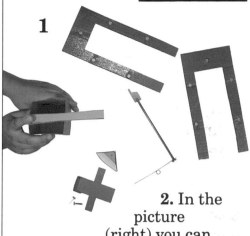

1. The frame for the pulley mechanism is made from two upside down U's of corrugated card 20cm tall and 8cm across , linked together with 5 straws. The see-saw and shoot are the same as the ones you made for the project on pages 26/27.

2. In the picture (right) you can see the basic shape for the see-saw with the cup to catch the marble. It is attached to the base with 2 paper-fasteners.

3. When you assemble the frame, first slide the four straws nearer to the bottom into their holes, then locate the top straw having put the cotton bobbin pulley in place already. When you are sure that the frame is rigid and level glue the straws to the frame.

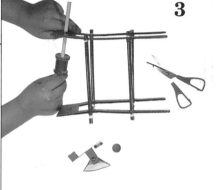

4. Cut the corner from a cereal box to provide the ramp shown in green below. Make sure that the shoot for the roller sticks out at the top of the ramp so that it tips the roller onto the ramp.

5. Glue two guides into place to channel the box which will carry the bobbin and attach a card built hammer with paper-fasteners. The box which carries the bobbin up is open at one side.

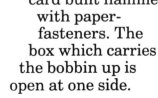

SCIENTIFIC TERMS

EFFORT The amount of work needed to mve an object, or load, over a distance.

ENERGY The capacity to do work. Energy can be stored and gradually released.

FORCE A push or a pull, equal to the product of mass and acceleration.

FULCRUM The pivot point of a lever.

FRICTION The force that resists movement when one surface moves relative to another.

GRAVITY The force that attracts objects to each other because of their mass. The more massive an object is, the greater its force of gravity.

LEVER In its simplest form, a rigid bar that pivots on its fulcrum or 'hinge'. Press down on one side, and the other side moves up.

LUBRICANT Oil or other matter used to make a surface smooth and to overcome friction.

PINION A small wheel that meshes with a larger one.

RESISTANCE The forces, such as gravity and friction which act upon objects, making them difficult to move. The greater the resistance, the greater the effort needed to move it.

WHEEL A disc-shaped object mounted on a central axle. The wheel is fixed to the axle or is free to spin on it.

WORK Measured in units called joules, work is equal to the force applied multiplied by the distance the load is moved.

INDEX